NOV 2013

Stark County District Library
www.StarkLibrary.org
330.452.0665

W9-AQG-078

DISCARDED

Map My Country

by Jennifer Boothroyd

first step nonfiction

Lerner Publications Company · Minneapolis

LERNER

SOURCE

Expand learning beyond the printed book. Download free, complementary educational resources for this book from our website, www.lerneresource.com.

Copyright © 2014 by Lerner Publishing Group, Inc.

All rights reserved. International copyright secured. No part of this book may be reproduced, stored in a retrieval system, or transmitted in any form or by any means—electronic, mechanical, photocopying, recording, or otherwise—without the prior written permission of Lerner Publishing Group, Inc., except for the inclusion of brief quotations in an acknowledged review.

The images in this book are used with the permission of: © JLP/Jose L. Pelaez/CORBIS, p. 4; © Laura Westlund/Independent Picture Service, pp. 5, 11, 12, 13, 15, 16, 17, 18, 19; © iStockphoto.com/Chris Schmidt, p. 6; © iStockphoto.com/Frank Cangelosi, p. 7; © iStockphoto.com/RTimages, p. 8; © Todd Strand/Independent Picture Service, pp. 9, 21; © Cultura Limited/SuperStock, p. 10; iStockphoto.com/ compucow, p. 14.

Front cover: © Laura Westlund/Independent Picture Service.

Main body text set in ITC Avant Garde Gothic Std Medium 21/25.
Typeface provided by Adobe Systems.

Lerner Publications Company
A division of Lerner Publishing Group, Inc.
241 First Avenue North
Minneapolis, MN 55401 U.S.A.

Website address: www.lernerbooks.com

Library of Congress Cataloging-in-Publication Data

Boothroyd, Jennifer, 1972–
    Map my country / by Jennifer Boothroyd.
       p.   cm. — (First step nonfiction - Map it out)
    Includes index.
    ISBN 978–1–4677–1113–5 (lib. bdg. : alk. paper)
    ISBN 978–1–4677–1738–0 (eBook)
    1. Cartography—Juvenile literature. 2. Maps—Juvenile literature. I. Title.
GA105.6.B64 2014
526—dc23   2012043291

Manufactured in the United States of America
1 – PP – 7/15/13

Table of Contents

We are learning about the
United States.

I have a map of the
country. It is **blank**.

A compass rose shows the four directions. They are
north, east, south, and west.

Alabama	Hawaii	Massachusetts	New Mexico	South Dakota
Alaska	Idaho	Michigan	New York	Tennessee
Arizona	Illinois	Minnesota	North Carolina	Texas
Arkansas	Indiana	Mississippi	North Dakota	Utah
California	Iowa	Missouri	Ohio	Vermont
Colorado	Kansas	Montana	Oklahoma	Virginia
Connecticut	Kentucky	Nebraska	Oregon	Washington
Delaware	Louisiana	Nevada	Pennsylvania	West Virginia
Florida	Maine	New Hampshire	Rhode Island	Wisconsin
Georgia	Maryland	New Jersey	South Carolina	Wyoming

This is a list of all the state names.

A computer will help me find each state's **location**.

I labeled Washington first.

Next, I labeled Florida.

It is tricky to label the smaller states.

Hawaii and Alaska are far away from the other states.

They have special spots on my map.

I colored the states I have
visited blue.

I colored states I want to
visit green.

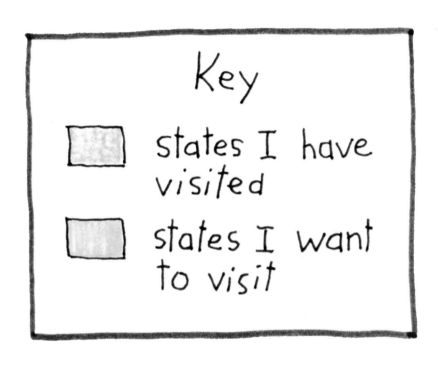

I made a map **key**. It tells what the colors mean.

I add my compass rose.
My map is done!

Fun Facts

- The United States started with 13 states. The country now has 50.

- Alaska has more land than any other state.

- Rhode Island has less land than any other state.

- More people live in Rhode Island than in Alaska!

- Washington, D.C., is a small area on the East Coast. It is not a state. It is our country's **capital**.

Glossary

blank – not filled in with details

capital – a place where the government is based

compass rose – a drawing showing the directions on a map

key – the part of a map that explains the meaning of certain colors or symbols on the map

location – where something is

Index

3 1333 04191 4787